About This Book

Every once in a while a book comes along that, in defiance of established literary rules, becomes an overwhelming success. Such a book is ANGEL UNAWARE.

Quietly it came upon the literary scene, catching the imagination and heart of the reading public. Letters began to pour in . . . newspapers and magazines reviewed it . . . Hollywood columnists gossiped about it . . . radio and television sang its praises. With its poignant, thought-provoking theme, this inspiring book skyrocketed into a runaway best seller.

Now, after 700,000 copies and 27 editions in hardcover, ANGEL UNAWARE is being published as an inexpensive paperback for the first time so that it may continue to be a living, heartwarming experience for millions throughout the world.

Dale Evans, the author of ANGEL UNAWARE, is well-known as the wife of the "King of the Cowboys," Roy Rogers. Dale Evans and Roy Rogers have been stars for more than 25 years— but they have much more than just stars. They have been an inspiration, by word and deed, to their millions of fans and friends around the world. This is because they are a living example of a way of life they believe in. ANGEL UNAWARE is dramatic proof of this.

Angel Unaware

By DALE EVANS ROGERS

FAMILY LIBRARY

E

NEW YORK

ANGEL UNAWARE

FAMILY LIBRARY
Published by arrangement with Fleming H. Revell Company

Tenth printing January, 1974

ISBN 0-515-00826-5

Printed in the United States of America

FAMILY LIBRARY is published by
Pyramid Publications, 919 Third Avenue,
New York, New York 10022, U.S.A.

Foreword to the paperback Edition

By Dale Evans

Although ten years have passed since her death, I sometimes feel that my beloved daughter, Robin, left our family only yesterday.

The memory of lovely Robin has never dimmed, nor has the pain of losing her diminished to any great degree. I have never wanted the pain of her loss to vanish. I have learned to live with it, and if there were no heartache left I honestly would have to confess that there was something seriously lacking in me as a woman and a mother.

I have but to close my eyes to picture my joy at Robin's birth when I was told that my husband, Roy Rogers, and I now had a baby daughter of our very own.

It didn't matter that Robin was not brought to me for the first two days after her birth. The explanation was that she had suffered a difficult beginning and was being given oxygen. When she finally came to my arms, the light fell on her sleeping face. I observed that she was very pretty but that her features had a slightly oriental look.

As Robin slept at my breast I explained this to

myself. I reminded myself that Roy's eyes were tilted slightly, as were his sister's and father's; it was a family characteristic because they were part Choctaw Indian.

The fact that Robin hardly moved at all and didn't cry failed to disturb me for my own mother had told me that I was a very lazy baby at first.

On Robin's second visit she squirmed a little as she snuggled next to me. I said to the nurse, "See, she'll be just like I was. I expect that in a few days she'll have had enough sleep and will be babbling a mile a minute before long. My mother," I explained laughingly, "says that once I started talking I never quit."

Tears came to the nurse's eyes. She turned away. Sudden anxiety stabbed at me.

"Something's wrong with my baby!" I cried. "Tell me, what is it?"

The nurse faced me, looking squarely in my eyes. "Mrs. Rogers," she said quietly, "I know you have the courage to take it. Make your doctor tell you." Then she fled from the room.

Half paralyzed with fear, I reached for the telephone and demanded to see my doctor. Soon, he was there with Roy. Only then did I learn that those close to me had not wanted me to face reality immediately. I had given birth to a borderline mongoloid child.

The truth was hard to grasp.

Roy and I were vaguely aware that mongolism

has been recognized for centuries but that the science of medicine has never been able to pinpo·nt the physical or chemical factors which cause the condition.

All we knew was that this couldn't, shouldn't be happening to us.

From the beginning, our fierce love for Robin would not allow us to listen to the advice of well-meaning friends who, with one voice, said, "You must send her to an inst·tution. She will be well cared for. You must not allow this tragedy to ruin your lives."

"She's ours," Roy said. "We love her and she's going to live with us as long as the Lord allows." That was that for both of us.

Looking back on that incredibly short time during which Robin blessed our lives, I must express gratitude for the understanding of many people. The press was particularly considerate and I shall be forever grateful. Although many reporters knew about Robin, not a line was published until we ourselves chose to make the facts known.

When I brought Robin home I told our children, Dusty and Linda Lou, that Robin would be slower to grow than other babies. I explained that she would never be able to do most of the things that other children enjoyed. Robin must be cared for like a delicate flower. They must always protect her.

Later I taught them that they must never look

or stare at a child who was in any way afflicted, but should remember that these children were God's special loved ones.

When Robin was nine months old we moved to the community of Encino in the San Fernando Valley section of Los Angeles. Here we enrolled the children in St. Nicholas Episcopal Church where the Rev. Harley Wright Smith, since retired, was pastor. Roy and I were Baptists, but we have always believed in attending our nearest neighborhood church, just as we do the Methodist church near our ranch now.

Roy and I had taken Robin to many doctors. Each diagnosis was more discouraging than the last. Robin had a large hole in her heart. No one would operate, although today medical science has made such tremendous progress that if she had lived she might have made great strides toward normality.

At the time, even in our sorrow, we treasured every moment with Robin. In her eyes we saw that she returned our love to us multiplied many times over.

One day Father Smith, whom I had not met, called on the telephone and said to me, simply, "I want you to understand that I know all about your child. You have done the right thing in bringing her home with you to cherish her and love her.

"You and your husband will soon begin to receive what our Lord wants you to learn from this child. In my opinion these little children are allowed to come into this word to bless lives. Their presence teaches patience and understanding that makes those around them more godly. Mrs. Rogers, you are truly blessed by the Lord, and you may be sure that your sweet Robin will one day be rewarded handsomely in the hereafter."

Father Smith, who baptized several of the Rogers children and grandchildren, was a towering man, not only physically but as a source of great strength to his parishoners. He never again spoke to me of Robin's condition, but he had planted the seed which before long was to lead my thoughts toward the writing of *Angel Unaware*.

When Robin was fifteen months old, Father Smith baptized her. To all outward appearances we were a normal, happy family.

Yet, in the privacy of our home we lived in constant concern for our fragile little darling. Her care was difficult. Nurses who were not up to the long hours of vigilance came and went. Roy and I grew stronger in our faith and in appreciation of the responsibility we had been given.

God has a way of compensating in all things and in all human beings. To the retarded and handicapped He gives a treasure few people ever attain. He gives them the double blessing of purity of thought and an amazing capacity for love.

I think the French best express what I want to

say. For centuries they have called these little children "those nearest to the heart of God."

These blessed ones can make only the most elemental of decisions for themselves if they are hungry or wish something in simple play. But is this really a handicap which should cause us to turn our backs on them? Isn't it wonderful to know that there are human beings amongst us who are incapable of being crafty or greedy? Should we not look with at least some sense of envy on those who will never attain the questionable freedom of knowledge which enables them to say, "I'm not sure I believe in God!"?

Robin, like most children, had many simple toys designed for those her age, but the gift she loved the most was a framed picture of Jesus carrying a lamb. The picture hung over her bed. She loved to look at it while I explained how Jesus loved little children. In those rare moments during which she struggled to communicate with Roy and me, she would turn in her crib, point to the picture and try to talk.

Near the end of her short life, Robin suffered an attack of the mumps, causing complications from which she never recovered. I recall the Sunday, one week before she died. Robin and I were in our breakfast nook, above which hung a lovely portrait of the face of Christ. I had been trying for more than an hour to give Robin nourishment, a bit of cracker and a taste of milk.

She refused the food and drink. I persisted, talking softly, trying to give her just anything that would supply energy to the fading little body to keep the spark of life alive. Finally, she turned her face away from me and wept. I was so concerned, I cried, too.

Then there was a little hand on my face. Robin looked at me, her eyes alight. From almost a prone position, she had raised herself with great effort so that she could point at the picture of Jesus. She seemed to be trying to comfort me. Soft sounds came from her lips. I knew that she was trying to tell me something, but I didn't know what it was.

All this is no figment of my imagination, and tears come to my eyes now as I write about the last hours of Robin's life here on earth. Could I then or now possibly question that she was a special creation of God?

If Robin had grown up as a normal child, she would now be fourteen years of age. I am sure she would have been a wonderful young person as all of our children have been, but I know that no matter how fine her life might have turned out to be, or how much she did for others she could not possibly have touched the lives of the many thousands she already has and still does today.

The real miracle of Robin began two days after her death. I had been sitting at the desk in our study for hours in the dazed aftermath which followed her passing, receiving endless calls of sympathy from friends. Suddenly things began to come into my mind so fast that I was hardly aware of the thoughts in a conscious manner. A pencil was in my hand and I began to write.

In the days that followed, little else was on my mind but the book I knew I had to write. Several times, while driving my car, a feeling or a thought would come to me so strongly that I would pull off to the side of the road and put the words to paper.

I am not dramatizing. This is exactly the way it all happened. If my life had depended upon it I never before could have written anything people would have wanted to read.

In six weeks the little book was finished. I prayed and committed *Angel Unaware* to God and to Robin. All of the royalties which would normally accrue to an author I pledged to the National Association for Retarded Children. For a time I kept track of the records but as the years have passed I am content only to know that many thousands of dollars have been contributed to the cause. And now that it is in this new edition I have again directed that the royalties be paid to deserving children, this time through the Exceptional Children's Foundation, 225 West Adams Street, in Los Angeles.

My rewards have come in many ways and on almost every day of my life since *Angel Unaware* was first published. Parents come up to me while I am shopping just to say, "Thank you for writing *Angel Unaware*. We have a child just like Robin, and the book has brought us happiness and faith we never had before."

After the book first appeared, Roy and I went on the road with our traveling show. Many people came backstage day after day with their handicapped children to see Trigger and to talk with Roy and me.

All this happened because we divulged the story of Robin. These sorrowing parents had new confidence because God had spoken to them through Robin and through us.

Besides the people we met personally there have been thousands during the past ten years who have written to me. To answer all the letters personally was impossible, so I devised a form letter advising anxious parents to contact their nearest minister, rabbi or priest and to get in touch with the parent groups in their community interested in the mentally retarded.

As many of the letters as I could, especially the desperate cases, were individually answered. In every case I advised the parents not to give up the child, not to shut their offspring out of their hearts even if the condition was such that a qualified institution was indicated.

I recall the essence of one letter in which I advised: "Go to see your child. Join in the program

prepared for him. Your grief will never be healed
by shutting yourself away, but only by being with
your child in mind and spirit. If you say, 'I will
put all of this away and out of my mind—it must
not wreck my life,' then it will wreck your life.
Accept what God has put in trust to you and you
will find the kind of happiness that those who
have not had our common experience can never
share."

Before Robin, neither Roy nor I really knew
anything about exceptional children. Ten years
ago it was a common practice for parents to put
them in institutions or keep them at home care-
fully out of sight.

In our visits to hospitals it was a joy to us to
seek out these children. We never saw the strange,
warped little bodies or distorted faces. We saw
only the light of love that shone from their eyes.

This year, in Seattle, a woman brought her
handicapped child to me and exclaimed, "This is
the first time she has been outside the house in
ten years." One little boy had been sent home
from the hospital the day before Roy and I visited
there. He was so despondent over having missed
us that he demanded to go back until Roy called
him on the telephone for a long chat.

A few years ago it was our privilege to be in-
vited as guests to the Annual Handycap Children's
Fishing Rodeo in Provo, Utah, where each year
the thoughtful people of that community prepare

a special picnic ground high in a canyon. Children are brought by bus to a mountain stream which is stocked with fish for the occasion. Wheel chairs are moved to the bank of the stream and even into the water so that the children may fish to their heart's content.

There were 500 children present the day we were there. We had wonderful fun, and I was delighted to hear from Elayne Schwartz, Television Editor of the Provo Daily Herald, that the event now attracts more than 1,000 children annually. Elayne conceived the original idea and she told me that the children persist in calling it the Roy Rogers Fishing Rodeo. When she reads these words I hope she will agree that if the name is to be changed we hope that it may become known as the Robin Rogers Fishing Rodeo, because had it not been for Robin, Roy and I might never have had the pleasure of meeting these wonderful children.

In closing, I would like to declare a few words of personal belief. My theory is that in this modern day we are all too tense and are living too fast. The exploding of atomic bombs which poison the air and must inevitably have crippling results on future generations—the consuming of tons of tranquilizing pills—these things were never intended by God to be visited on future generations.

Still, there is hope. I have told parent after parent not to give up hope, for help may be at hand. For example, only recently at UCLA Medical Center a boy with a heart condition very similar to Robin's survived a delicate operation and now has a chance for the future.

Remember, in this century the science of medicine has found cures for pneumonia and tuberculosis. Tomorrow dedicated men may begin to find important answers for the mentally retarded and otherwise handicapped child.

Parents should never give up. If their child does not survive to live a normal life, as was the case with our beloved Robin, let the child bless their lives, enrich their lives in understanding, compassion and the joy that comes with serving the unfortunate.

Above all, never give up hope.

Gratefully,

March, 1963

Dale Evans Rogers

The House of Rogers

by Norman Vincent Peale

ELIZABETH (my ten-year-old daughter) and I had
been all-out fans of Roy Rogers and Dale Evans
long before we knew them as personal friends. We
loved their movie and TV adventures, but that
wasn't all; we sensed something fine and whole-
some in what they said and did, in their dynamic
personalities, in the radiant joy and lovable humil-
ity which is so much a part of them.

Then they started coming to New York for their
Rodeo in Madison Square Garden, and every Sunday morning I saw them in my congregation at
Marble Collegiate Church. We returned the com-
pliment by attending the Rodeo. We were thrilled
as they raced about the arena and as Roy sang
"Peace in the Valley"—a song that is half ballad
and half hymn. But we were moved deeply when
he said to the youngsters in *his* "Congregation," "I
hear some kid says it is sissy stuff to go to Sunday
school. Don't you believe him. Sunday school is
for he-men." The awe with which the children
accepted this convinced me that cowboys are

often more effective preachers than the preachers themselves.

Their business is entertainment; their purpose is to speak for God in their daily work. By their words, their kindliness and their uprightness and their love of people, they turn the mind of everyone they meet to God—a rare and beautiful accomplishment, in our kind of world!

Dale Evans does just that, in this little book. She is a mother who has won great victory over great sorrow. When she first told me the story you will read here, I realized that I was hearing of an amazing experience and standing in the presence of a great soul. I saw at once that Robin, her baby, had not lived and died in vain. Where most babies die and leave the mother crushed, Robin put on immortality and her mother found the very joy of God in what might otherwise have been an overwhelming tragedy.

The sweetness, the touching humor and spiritual understanding with which little Robin Rogers talks with God in this book will comfort and strengthen all who read it, as it did me when I read the manuscript—through misty eyes.

This is one book I'll never forget.

Foreword

This is the story of what a baby girl named Robin Elizabeth accomplished in transforming the lives of the Roy Rogers family.

Our baby came into the world with an appalling handicap, as you will discover when you read her story.

I believe with all my heart that God sent her on a two-year mission to our household, to strengthen us spiritually and to draw us closer together in the knowledge and love and fellowship of God.

It has been said that tragedy and sorrow never leave us where they find us. In this instance, both Roy and I are grateful to God for the privilege of learning some great lessons of truth through His tiny messenger, Robin Elizabeth Rogers.

This is Robin's story. This is what I, her mother, believe she told our Heavenly Father shortly after eight p. m. on August 24, 1952.

Dale Evans Rogers

*Be not forgetful to entertain
strangers: for thereby some have
entertained angels unawares*
                    Hebrews 13:2

OH, FATHER, it's good to be home again. I thought
sometimes that You had forgotten me, Down
There. Two years Up Here doesn't seem like
much, but on earth it can be a long, long time—
and it was long, and often hard, for all of us.

When You lifted me up from the earth, just a
few minutes ago, it was Sunday, and my Mommy
and Daddy were crying, and everything seemed
so dark and sad and confused. And all of a sudden
it was bright and clear and happy, and I was in
Your arms. Was it the same way for them Down
There, Father? You can put me down, now; I'm
perfectly all right, now that I'm rid of that lump
of hindering clay. . . .

That music sounds nice—it's even nicer than the
music I heard Down There. I guess a lot of people didn't know it, but Down There I had as
much music as I had pain. I had my own little
red radio, and my nurse let me play it whenever
I wanted to. And I had the sweetest little white
wooley horse, with tunes in his tummy, and he

played for me every night on my pillow, right before I went to sleep. Of course, I loved horses, maybe because Daddy was a cowboy and loved them, too.

Mommy often took me in to play on the big piano, and I had a little toy piano, too, that I used to pound day and night. It helped.

Yes, there was music. I even heard happy songs that they couldn't hear. They just saw my sickness, and they felt sorry for me. But I knew *why* I was sick, and that because I was sick I could do things for them; and as they say Down There, that was "music to my ears."

It was quite an experience, Father. When You sent me on that earthly mission, I never dreamed what it would be like, or how much We could do, in two short years. We did a lot.

WELL, ON August 26, 1950 (earth time) I woke up in a place they called a "hospital," and I could see people in white robes standing all around. Just like it is Up Here, Father—white robes all around. One of them, a nurse, said, "She's blue." I didn't know what that meant, but I did know that everything was going according to the Plan. They said something about a cord being wrapped around my neck, and they slipped that off, and I felt more comfortable. They spanked me a little to make me cry (and laughed while they did it!), and then they put me in a funny little thing called an "oxygen box," and the doctor turned away from me to help the woman on the table. That was my earthly mother.

She opened her eyes and turned to look at me, and she said, "Hi, Robin. You're beautiful!" Then they wheeled her out to her own room, to rest.

The doctor came back to me and looked at me, hard. He seemed so worried about me that I started worrying about *him*. Some other doctors and nurses came and stood looking down at me and whispering among themselves, and they started doing all sorts of odd things to me to make me move around.

They told each other that something was wrong, because I didn't "respond" to their "tests" like the other babies did. Poor souls! I could have told them that this, too, was part of the Plan. But they couldn't know that—they didn't have eyes to see You there beside me, or ears to hear Your voice.

They didn't realize that You provide certain conditions in order to accomplish some wonderful purpose. A lot of them Down There don't understand yet, Father, that You always have a blessing in mind, in everything You plan. Many mothers, with babies like me, wouldn't be so bitter and so heart-broken if they just knew You and Your ways better.

The doctor who "delivered" me came back. (I like that word "delivered"; it makes the doctors seem like Your Agents, or Your "mail-men" Down

There.) He brought three children's doctors (called "pediatricians")—and how they did talk! And shake their heads! I heard one of the nurses say, "She has Mongoloid eyes." I wondered what Mongoloid meant. They seemed to think it was something awful.

Art Rush was there, too; he's Daddy's manager and closest friend, and he said, "So what? There's nothing unusual about that. Her Daddy has almond-shaped eyes, and he's not ashamed of them, and his father and his grandfather had them. It runs in the family." There was quite an argument about all this, but I didn't take much interest in it. Why should I worry? I knew it had all been arranged. . . .

I had a pretty hard time getting started; they had to give me oxygen for the first few days.

I guess Mommy didn't know about all this fuss, because when they took me in to see her, she was so happy. She patted my face and kissed me over and over and one day she prayed to You, while she held me in her arms, and promised You that she would help me to grow up to be a good Christian. I liked that. I knew We were on the right track.

Daddy came at visiting hours, and stood looking at me through the glass, laughing and jumping all around, and making funny signs, and looking proud. I heard him say once that I had little ears, like Mommy's. They were happy about me, all right.

BUT THE doctors and nurses weren't so happy. They were all dreading the time when they'd have to tell Mommy and Daddy about the bad shape I was in. Whenever Mommy got to boasting about me to her nurse, the nurse would change the subject. That happened several times, and Mommy began to get suspicious. Finally she asked the nurse right out if there was anything wrong with me, and the nurse looked away and said she wasn't allowed to discuss my "condition."

One day the nurse slipped; she said that the doctor had said something about my being a "borderline" baby. Mommy's face went white, and she asked the nurse, "Did he say . . . *Mongoloid?*" I felt so sorry for that nurse! She didn't know what to say then, and she tried to make the best of it by saying, "Don't be worried. There is only a thin line between genius and insanity. Some handicapped children have turned out to be exceptionally brilliant. They can go—either way."

When the doctor came, Mommy went for him! He was a good doctor; he had a big heart under that white coat. He said he wasn't just sure yet, and he hadn't said anything to Mommy because he didn't want to worry her before she got on her feet, but I hadn't responded very well to *some* of their tests. Otherwise I was "all right"—and I had rallied quite well in the last two days. But my "muscle-tone" was poor, I had trouble swallowing my food, and I seemed to be listless. He said that symptoms like these, at birth, *sometimes* meant the baby might not develop as it should.

Mommy asked him what she and Daddy should do. What did anybody do with a Mongoloid baby? Doctor said gently that there wasn't much anyone could do; the few institutions for such babies were overcrowded, and the State homes and hospitals wouldn't take in "one of these children" until he was four years old. Then he said something fine:

"Take her home and love her. Love will help more than anything else in a situation like this—more than all the hospitals and all the medical science in the world." That's one thing I learned Down There, Father—that the doctors are just beginning to discover how much help You are in *any* situation. They're beginning to talk seriously about "tender, loving care." You are getting through to the doctors.

When the doctor left, Mommy started to cry. She said there should be *some* place for babies like me. Why didn't somebody do something about it? Maybe—and my heart missed a beat when I heard her say it—maybe it was high time the Rogers did something about starting a Foundation for handicapped babies. I loved that—not because it could help me, but because it looked like the first fruit of my mission Down There. Because I had come to them, they were already planning to help others like me!

But Mommy kept on crying, and Daddy said, "Don't cry. God will take care of her; she's in His hands, and His hands are big enough to hold her. We will pray, and trust Him."

That was just like my Daddy. He has always trusted You, but You know, he did get to wondering sometimes. He didn't doubt that everything was being taken care of from Up Here—not that. Daddy had been a Christian for some time before I came, but like most people Down There, he saw things that hurt his heart, and he couldn't help asking questions.

It always hurt him to see little crippled children, and he'd ask, "Why? *Why*? Where's God? I know He's a loving God, but if He loves these children, why does He let them suffer?" A lot of folks ask these questions, Father, and a lot of them never seem to get any answers. Daddy did!

He began to read his Bible, as though he had never seen it before. And he prayed, more and more often. I could see the change in his face; it was quiet now. He seemed to be getting hold of himself. We were getting to him, Father; a new Roy Rogers was being born.

They took me "home," to the house in the Hollywood Hills.

THERE WAS a sweet nurse, named Donna, waiting for me, when we got home—and the three brothers and sisters You sent on ahead of me. My brother Dusty ran up to the nurse who was holding me and said, "Can I see the baby?" He put his finger on my forehead and asked, "Is she real?" And Cheryl and Linda laughed and cooed over me and said the nicest things to me, and they thought I was wonderful. They didn't see anything wrong. Children never do. They have clear, sharp eyes that look 'way down, and what they see is always beautiful.

Donna was like that, too; she had brought Dusty through the first six months of his life, and she kept telling Mother and Daddy that I was going to be all right. She was speaking the truth, and didn't realize it! Once she asked Mommy if "R-H Negative Blood Factor" had anything to do with the way I turned blue when I tried to take milk out of the bottle. Mommy said the doctors had told her that the R-H Factor had nothing to do with my condition.

Poor Donna slipped and fell and broke her wrist, so another sweet, motherly nurse named "Jo" came to take care of me.

They put me in a contraption called a "bassinet," and tried hard to make me drink that milk. I had a hard time of it; I couldn't seem to get suction enough. It made me so tired, and my whole left arm would turn blue. And my head was wobbly as anything! I just couldn't seem to control it. Mommy worried over that; they almost had to tie her in bed to keep her from coming in and standing over me, looking anxious.

The milk business was bad enough, but when I was three weeks old a doctor examined me and found that I had developed a heart murmur. He said he was afraid of that; it was just another "Mongoloid symptom." He said he always advised parents, in situations like this, to put the baby in a "home"; they'd have to give the child up sometime, anyway, and it was easier to do it quickly, before the child became entrenched in their hearts. He said that mothers gave children like this all their attention, and were likely to neglect the other children in the family. He was a kind man, and he meant well, but what he said left Mommy so stunned she couldn't answer.

Daddy said, "No! We'll keep her and do all we can for her, and take our chances." Mommy smiled then; she was glad, and she said what I had been waiting to hear her say: that You had sent me for some special reason, and they had no right to cast aside anything or anyone You had sent.

She said she was sorry for other parents who had babies like me. Father, it *is* hard. It was hard for Daddy and Mommy—but worth every tear and heartache it cost! I saw what was happening: already, they were beginning to appreciate Your Cross. . . .

Mommy kept trying to make me smile. The pediatrician kept asking her, "Has she smiled yet?" He said if a baby didn't smile until he was three months old, it meant that he was at least fifty per cent retarded in his mental growth. Mommy didn't want to leave me, for anything, until she saw that smile

Oh, Father, she and Jo tried so hard to make me smile! Mommy worked overtime on that. I was never out of her thoughts. She was too "possessive" about me, and that wasn't good.

Of course, there was a reason for that. Mommy had always been "career-minded." Even when she was a young girl she wanted to succeed, and succeed *big*, in show business, and for a long time she put that career before everything else in her life. But after I arrived, it didn't seem to mean so much to her, after all.

We took care of that "success" business in short order, didn't We? She seemed to be trying to push all thought of her career out of her mind, so as to have more room in her mind for me. She was always praying for me, always hovering over me. Then she realized that giving me all her time and attention might be bad, too; there were other children in the house, and it wasn't fair to them. She tried to share her time and her love with Dusty and Cheryl and Linda and Daddy, and to go on with her work.

It was quite a struggle she went through, trying to find out what You wanted her to do about all this. You used a mighty hot fire in purging her for Our use, Father, but the flame was healing, too.

Daddy was trying to learn, too.

Just before they left to go on the tour, Daddy came into my room with a funny-looking thing called a "camera." He ran the window-shades up high; Your sun hit my weak eyes full force, and I set up quite a howl. Daddy went ahead and took a lot of pictures of me; he loved pictures and cameras. He wasn't satisfied to take pictures inside; he had to take me out on the porch, and "shoot" some more.

He was a lot of fun, my Daddy—everybody loved him Down There. He was so young in spirit—just like a boy—and after I came he seemed younger than ever. You wouldn't believe it, but he was often shy and nervous when he faced crowds. But not after he got to reading his Bible and studying me! After awhile he was relaxed, and confident, and sure of himself, and not nervous at all. I think it was because he came to understand that Your arms were always beneath him, as they were beneath me, and that You wouldn't let either one of us fall.

I loved him the first time I saw him, and many a time I wished I could have a heart-to-heart talk with him, because he was trying so hard to find out what You had in mind. I think he'd been trying to find out about that before We went to work on him, because once I heard him say that his big success came to him because of all the letters he got from boys and girls, saying they prayed for him. Now his idea of success was changing; We were teaching him that real success was *spiritual*.

He was changing, all right. The old question about why God let innocent children suffer didn't seem to bother him very much, any more. Bless his heart, he was learning that it isn't really we innocent children who suffer, it's the ones around us who suffer while they're learning how to be obedient to Your will.

Mommy was always trying to figure it out—to find some reason for my "affliction." Sometimes she said maybe it was part of the Plan to send Daddy and her an afflicted child so Daddy could understand all afflicted children; other times she thought it was because of some old sin or sins— and then she would think of some wonderful Christian having the same trouble she was having, and she'd ask, "Why?" and get all mixed up again.

But getting mixed up a little doesn't matter, does it, Father? Anybody who thinks get confused, sooner or later. But I noticed Down There that those who tried to think out things about You and Your ways usually found a way out of their confusion. It was those who didn't care enough to think at all that I felt sorry for. I always thought it was the not caring and not thinking that was sinful, not the being confused.

When I was two months old, my parents had to go off on one of those "personal appearance" tours, and they took me out to Jo's house, where it was nice and dry and sunny. It was cold and damp in Hollywood Hills, and Mommy didn't think that would be good for me. She and Daddy were finishing up a "recording" of a radio broadcast, but they came out to see me the very next day.

That day there was a consultation with two doctors. They said I had a very bad heart condition, and that I probably wouldn't live very long, but for Mommy and Daddy to go ahead with the tour, because nothing would happen for six months, anyway. Mommy asked why they couldn't operate on my heart, and they said no operation could help.

When she heard that, Mommy cried; Daddy told her again, "It's up to God now. Let's leave it with Him." Mommy said she knew that—but she would fight to the last ditch to help me until You called for me. Of course, she was still fighting herself. . . .

I'm glad they had to go on that tour—glad they had to go out and entertain people, because while they were so busy making those other people happy they wouldn't worry about me. Up Here we know that if we want to be happy we have to make others happy; Down There, they haven't quite caught up with that idea. But they will.

I guess Mommy would have collapsed if it

hadn't been for that rule that "the show must go on."

They called every night while they were away; Mommy was overjoyed the night Jo told her that I had "laughed right out loud," that day. Everybody in the house laughed with me, they were so glad—my aunts and grandparents and brother and sisters and Ginny, Dusty's nurse, and our nice housekeeper, Emily. They were good to me—so good that sometimes I got to wishing my mission could go on a little longer. But every time that happened—every time I got "earth-minded"—I would start thinking of You, and of how nice it was Up Here. That was when they said I had "a far-away look" in my eyes, and they'd try to snap me out of it. It *was* a far-away look; I was seeing things they couldn't see, and I pitied them. Some day they'll know; some day they'll see clearly, instead of in their misty mirrors.

They loved me, all of them, and maybe when I laughed it was in joy and thankfulness for their love. They weren't ashamed of their little "borderline" Mongoloid! A lot of parents are, You know. They whisk them off somewhere to keep them hidden, so others won't know. That's partly because they want to shelter these children from the eyes of the curious people, and partly it's because of their own pride.

Pride! I got so sick of that, Down There. It's an ugly weed, Father, growing all over the place.

And there's nothing like having a handicapped child to strip the pride and pretense from a pair of parents. I guess it's all right for a father to throw out his chest and boast about how smart his boy Jim is, but it's wrong when he tries to send thanks Up Here because his children are just a little better than any other children. It's really good when You send a handicapped baby to people like that; it takes them down a peg or two, and their real character begins to show, and they begin to be the kind of people You want them to be.

Mommy and Daddy went to one of the finest medical clinics in the world, during this tour, and they showed the top man my picture, and told him what the other doctors had said. He took one look, and asked, "Is she a good baby?"

"Oh, yes!" said Mommy.

"And is she always in a relaxed position, like this picture shows?"

"Most of the time, yes."

"Then you have a real problem," he said. "There's absolutely nothing we can do—for the heart, or for anything else. *There is no help.*"

He told Mommy that this affliction was no respecter of persons, that it hits anywhere, any time. One of his friends, a top baby doctor, had a baby just like me. He advised Mommy to put me in a home, before her heart broke.

Mommy wouldn't listen to it. I'm glad she

didn't, because if she had, she and Daddy might have missed Your point completely.

THE DAY before they got home, Jo got a "virus," and had to leave me. Daddy and Mommy came "on the double," scared half out of their wits that I'd get the virus, too, and they started hunting for a new nurse. They had to record another radio broadcast that week, so You can imagine the confusion around the house. Mommy called doctors, hospitals, nurses agencies—everything, and no nurse could be found, for love or money. They were really scared, for I was hard to feed, and my head seemed more wobbly than ever. But they found a nurse. Funny, isn't it, how things always work out, Down There? People fall all over themselves while You're working it out. . . .

Art Rush (that's Daddy's manager, remember?) called up and said he knew a lady who could help me. They sent for her, and she came and talked to Mommy and told her I could be healed, no matter what the doctors said—that God could do that. She said she knew a nurse who would take me, but Mommy would have to consent to having me live at the nurse's house for a few months—where she wouldn't have to contend with Mommy's fearful thoughts about me. She said that babies felt fear, that Mommy was putting her fear into me, and that would hold me back.

You can imagine what Mommy said. NO! A big,

loud, furious NO! She sat down and began telephoning all over, looking for another nurse. Of course she didn't find one. She wasn't supposed to, according to the Plan. . . .

Finally she said, "Oh, all right. But this nurse will have to spend a few days at our house first, so we can see how she and Robin get along."

So the new nurse came; I called her "Cau-Cau," and she took charge of me just like she'd known me all my life. Mommy relaxed, and let me go.

Cau-Cau knew her business about babies. She told Mommy I wasn't really her child; I was God's child. She said I was with You before I came to her, and that Mommy should be glad to give me back to You, and that You'd take care of me.

The lady who got this nurse for Mommy said the same thing; and she said that Mommy should never think of me as an imperfect child, but as a child perfect in Your eyes.

They were part of the Plan, all right. They were doing just what You sent them to do.

I SHARED a nice sunny room with Cau-Cau, in her home, and I began to feel better. I was stronger, and while I couldn't sit up, my head was steadier, and I was beginning to take some interest in things around me. But I was still pretty nervous; whenever anyone raised his voice, I started to cry. Any noise bothered me.

Father, it's so *noisy* Down There. So much babble and silly racket. What are they trying to do, anyway? Are they noisy because they're afraid of something, or what?

They worried about my "coordination," which certainly wasn't too good. From the time I began to notice bright objects, they would try to make me pick up rattles and toys. You should have heard Mommy the day she was writing down a telephone number, and I grabbed the pencil out of her hand, and started scribbling all over the notebook. Right away, she got me crayons and a big drawing book, to encourage me. She bubbled over every time I showed the least sign of improvement. She was still hoping. . . .

Cau-Cau used to say that I had "such loving hands . . . always stretched out to give . . . not earthly, grasping hands, and that's heavenly!" Of course, my hands were loving. They were filled with Your love, so they could bless those around me.

She and Mommy were worried about my little narrow foot. Cau-Cau said they would have to have my shoes "specially made." I had to choke down a giggle, because Up Here we don't need "specially made shoes" at all. Matter of fact, we don't need anything, Here. What a blessing that is!

Humans worry too much. If they could somehow trust more and worry less, they'd have heaven on earth, wouldn't they? I wanted to talk to them about that, and sometimes I got so anxious about it that I would start to jabber, a mile a minute. They would stare at me, and try to understand what I was trying to say, and—forgive me, Father, but I'm afraid I lost my patience with them. You know, I loved them, and I wanted to have them understand, and I hated to see them groping.

Mommy used to hold me on her lap to listen to a religious program on the radio; I heard her whisper that she hoped I'd "somehow understand." Poor heart—if she only knew how much I understood!

It seemed like *everybody* came out to see me on my first Christmas. Mommy brought me a doll in a bright red dress, and I loved it. My grandfather and grandmother and my uncle came, too, and there were my great big grown-up brother Tom, and his wife, Barbara. He had the kindest eyes; I looked in those eyes and saw You.

They all played with me until I got pretty tired, and started to perspire, and nurse said they'd better go. They all had tears in their eyes when they left, and I wanted to cheer them up. I wanted to say, "This is Christmas, and you should be glad. The angels sang for the Babe in the manger, and they're singing for me. Can't you hear it? *Listen!*" But my balky old tongue wouldn't behave. . . .

Mommy came to see me almost every day, and I don't think Cau-Cau approved of that, but she couldn't do anything about it. Mommy said she intended to see me whenever she had the chance. And she said our family was moving out to a ranch at Encino, in the valley, and she was going to build a little house for me and Cau-Cau, because she wanted me at home.

Cau-Cau said she'd come, "for a little while, until Robin gets used to living with all those people," and Daddy and Grampy and my great uncle started building it right away. . . .

I was ten months old when we moved into that house. It was pretty, with two rooms and a bath; my room was blue, like my eyes, and there were frilly white curtains at the windows. It made you happy just to look at it.

The new ranch was really something. Daddy had lots of dogs, and Cau-Cau would wheel me out in my go-cart to see them. And there were chickens and ducks and horses and even little foxes and raccoons. I got to know one dog real well; her name was Lana, and when I was fretty or nervous she'd come up and nuzzle me with her cold nose, and I'd feel better. Her fur was a soft gray color, like a dove's, and she had long silky ears that I couldn't help pulling whenever I got my hands on them. Lana didn't mind. Everywhere I went, she followed me.

Funny, about that. Children and animals Down There get along fine. They sort of talk to each other. . . .

We had some geese, and were they a noisy bunch! They made a queer hissing sound whenever we came near them, and I learned to make it, too; Cau-Cau thought that was smart of me, and she told me so. Some days Cau-Cau would give me a piece of stale bread to feed the chickens, or we'd take a walk over to the next ranch where there was a gentle old horse I loved, and I'd pat his nose, and he'd whinny back to me in horse language.

Cau-Cau read animal books to me at mealtime. That way, I got through the meals. They were hard to take, Father. I never cared much for solid food, and they played all sorts of tricks on me to get me to eat it. Finally they got me a suction-bottom plate and a specially curved spoon, hoping I might find my mouth with it. Every now and then, I did! It was an awful bore, and I got it over with as quickly as possible. It was easier in the mornings, when I was hungry; I was so cranky then that Cau-Cau called me "an impatient little witch." She was right. I was.

When I was bored I'd cry. Mommy couldn't stand that; she was afraid it would affect my weak heart. But Daddy said it was normal, or "O.K.," for a baby to cry.

My head was a little more "normal" now; I could control it a little better, and I was doing better with my tongue, too. And my legs! I could do things with my legs. From the time I was six months old I could lift them up straight over my head, and throw them out sideways—"doing the splits," Daddy called it. The doctor was afraid I'd throw my hips out of joint doing the splits, so he put a brace between my feet. I know this was supposed to keep me from hurting myself, but how I hated that brace! It made me more nervous than ever. I had to wear that brace constantly during the last four months I was Down There, and it wasn't fun.

They kept praying for me. You know, Father, *thousands* of people, scattered all over the country, prayed for me. One way or another, they heard about me, and they talked to You about me. Once, the whole big Southern Baptist Convention, in San Francisco, prayed. Didn't You like that?

They had "round table" prayers in the home, and it pleased me so that I just couldn't keep quiet. I tried to say the words with them, but the words got all mixed up. But they never scolded me. Seems as though they knew all along I was an angel. . . .

After dinner, Mommy would take me to the big piano and let me play. I tried hard to say "play piano," but it wouldn't come, and the best I could say was "pah-pah." Mommy would play and sing for me, and I used to take her hand and make her play some more; then Cau-Cau would say "Bed time!", and I'd throw them all a kiss, and nurse and Mommy tucked me in. I always hated to leave that piano.

Maybe I'm talking too much about myself, and not enough about what was happening to Mommy and Daddy. I could see that they were "growing in grace." I heard Mommy say one day that she was coming to believe that the only important thing in this world was a person's relationship to God and his faith in Jesus Christ. Then she said she was actually grateful to You for sending me in my handicapped condition, because I had made her walk closer to You. She was always reading her Bible, and when she went off with Daddy to San Francisco to testify to Your love in that big convention, I was proud of them. They were not just talking; they were practicing.

And Daddy! He was more and more interested in *sick* children, and he tried to get to see every sick boy or girl who called for him. They loved him. He wore a big white cowboy hat with a silver band on it—I used to put it on and play peek-a-boo with him. He got to calling me "Little Angel" —and I knew then that he knew.

MOMMY AND DADDY worked hard. They left us for two whole weeks, to go "on location" for a series of television pictures; Daddy had an accident while he was riding horseback, and we even heard that he'd been killed. Of course he wasn't, but it upset everybody for a little. Down There, Father, bad news travels twice as fast as good news. Why is that? Shouldn't it be the other way 'round?

They were busy making motion pictures from sunrise to sunset—so busy that I wondered whether it was worth their while. Why work so hard just to make a little money, and then die?

Then one day I overheard Mommy say something about their work that I hadn't heard them ever say before: she said that if they could get Your message to people, especially to young people, through their movies and television and rodeos—if they could just get in a good word for You this way, it was worth all the hard work. And I watched that idea grow and grow and *grow* in their hearts, all during Our mission.

My first earth birthday came along, and we had a great party. Everybody gave me the nicest presents. I had a cake, and Mommy had a photographer come out and take my picture. The present I liked best was a picture of Jesus holding a little blond girl in His arms, and mothers holding their babies up for You to bless. It made me so homesick! Mommy hung it at the head of my bed, so that I could see it before going to sleep, and the first thing in the morning when I woke up. She tried to teach me to say "Jesus," but all I could get out was "tay-tay."

Cau-Cau gave me a wonderful present, and she never knew it. She told Mommy that of all the babies she had nursed, she loved me most, because I needed her most, and she said I was teaching her to be patient. I laughed and kicked my feet when she said that; I saw the lessons soaking in, all around.

I WAS STANDING up most of the time, right then, in nurse's lap, and everybody was so happy about it. But all of a sudden I was awfully sick, and it looked for awhile as though my mission was over. I had a "convulsion"; it took me a long time to get over that and when I did, my legs wouldn't hold me up. I couldn't stand up any more.

Mommy and Daddy were sad about that—but they kept right on, as though nothing had happened. At Christmas we had the happiest party (this was my *second* Christmas); that was when I got my little red piano. Mommy and Daddy went to a midnight service to thank You for sending me.

Sometimes, it seemed that every day was Christmas, at least to me. They would sit me up in the middle of a big play table and let me roll a lot of brightly-colored balls around; I could throw them, Daddy said, "like a big league pitcher." Even when they took me to the "orthopedic" place, to have my "physical therapy," I had fun; I would take a round disk and fit it over a rounded piece of wood, and Mommy would play "catch" with the disks and do all sorts of things to keep me interested, so I would try to stand up. I got so I could stand for five whole minutes.

Cheryl, my oldest sister, played the piano. She had studied only a few months, but she could play almost anything at first sight. I loved to sit on her lap while she played fast, happy music. It would excite me so much that I'd grab her hands to make her play faster. . . .

They all laughed at me when I watched the ice skaters on television; I'd sway with them, and when the skaters came up close on the screen, I'd wave to them. It was all done silently—but what voices there were in that silence, for me!

Emily, our housekeeper, laughed over the wrist watch business. I had a weakness for wrist watches, and when Emily would say, "What time is it, Robin?" I'd hold up my wrist to her, just like I was wearing one. Emily played peek-a-boo with me, over her coffee cup. She seemed to see something, deep, in me. . . .

WELL, Spring came, nice and warm, and with Spring came Nancy. You know Nancy—she's Your other little angel who lives near us. She's ten now, and going strong on *her* mission. She's had thirty-five operations on her legs, but oh, Father, how happy she is, and how happy she's made the people around her! When I saw her, I saw You again, and I felt all warm and good inside. Nancy has lifted her own mother up for a new fresh look into heaven—and she has helped lift my own Mommy, too.

I was so glad to learn that You had introduced Nancy to Mommy before I got there; she'd been a "fan" of Mommy's and Daddy's for some time, and a good friend of my sisters, Linda and Cheryl. Nancy's mother looked at me and she said, "Robin is straight from heaven. I see it in her eyes—just as I see it in Nancy's."

She told Mommy that I had a great work to do Down There, and that she and Daddy were lucky to have a part in that work. She also told Mommy about a doctor "up north" who had helped little children like me, and Mommy said she'd take Cau-Cau and me to see him just as soon as they got back from a rodeo engagement in Houston, Texas.

Just as soon as they got back. They knew I'd be there when they got back.

They had me "christened" before they left for Houston, because to Mommy, right at this particular time, it seemed more important than anything else in the world to have me dedicated to You. So they made arrangements with the minister, dressed me up in a white organdy dress (fit for an angel!) with a pink sash, and some new white shoes, and Cau-Cau curled my hair and put a ribbon on my "topknot" (a sort of halo, You know), and away we went.

Art Rush was there; he said he wouldn't miss *this* for anything. And nurse went along, too. I think I got the greatest thrill of all when the minister reached out and took me in his arms. Mommy gave me to him so gladly; she seemed to be saying in her heart, "Here she is, God. I give her to You. I won't fight any more; I won't try to keep her so much to myself. She's Yours. Take her."

The minister took me in his arms and held me, and I looked up into that kind, patient, loving face and saw You again. Mommy and Daddy were so happy about it that I knew *they* knew You were standing there with them.

Then Mommy and Daddy went off to the Houston rodeo—and what a show that turned out to be! You know, Daddy comes tearing out into the arena on Trigger, and the kids all shout and howl and cheer, and then Daddy talks to them. He tells them never to get the idea in their little heads that there's anything sissy about going to Sunday school and church. He'll ask, "Now let's give a big hand to everybody who's going to church on Sunday!" In a *rodeo*, Father! Rodeos are supposed to be tough, and wild and woolly. Daddy makes them something a lot finer than that.

Even in that big Madison Square Garden, in New York City, he gets down off Trigger and sings a song about Peace, and it's so quiet You can hear a pin drop, even though You're way off Up Here in heaven. They really listen when Daddy sings about "Peace in the Valley":

Oh, I'm tired and I'm weary, but I must
    travel on
Till the Lord comes and calls me, calls
    me away,
Where the morning is bright, and the
    Lamb is the light,
And the night is as fair as the day.
    There will be peace in the Valley for me,
    ... peace in the Valley for me.

I wonder if Daddy is thinking of *his* peace, or
mine, when he sings that?

    There's no sadness, no sorrow, no trouble
        I see!
    There'll be peace in the Valley for me!

No sadness, no sorrow! No crippled children,
Father!

    There the bear will be gentle and the
        wolf will be tame
    And the lion will lie down with the lamb;
    There the host from the wild will be led
        by a child ...

A child like *me*, Father?

    And I'll be changed from this creature
        that I am.

Mommy said Daddy had never sung that song so beautifully as he sang it in Houston, and Daddy said that was because it was Your song, not his, and that You were helping him sing it. He had peace—perfect peace. He and Mommy went to a big church in Houston on Sunday, and told the folks about it.

They were coming along, Father.

WE GOT READY to go to see the doctor up north— in San Francisco. Just before we left, Mommy took me to a "heart specialist," to see what he would say about that tricky heart of mine. It wasn't that she was looking for miracles to happen, Father; it was just that she thought she should do *everything* to help me, and she thought that it might be Your will to reach down to me through some doctor's hand, and make it easier for me.

But—no. That wasn't the way it was to be. The doctor said my heart was already enlarged, seriously, and that they couldn't possibly operate. By the end of the summer, he said, that condition would be "important," and they were to bring me to him again.

Mommy asked this doctor about the doctor in San Francisco, and he said, "I hate to see you go on chasing rainbows like this, but I know you will, so go ahead." We went ahead.

We had a room high up in a hotel, and they

had one of those "air raid warnings" while we were there, and I'll never forget it. I thought those whistles would burst my ear drums. How they do make noise, and how people do scamper around like a lot of frightened ants! I just couldn't understand it. Maybe you can explain it to me later, Father. *Why* do they act like that, Down There? It's so foolish to go out of your way to get scared, and to create confusion. I listened to the whistles and the shouting, and I thought of Daddy singing Your song about Peace, and I asked myself, "What's wrong Down Here, anyway? Why don't they just get Your peace?" Nobody seemed to know. They just went on. . . .

The doctor was a kind man, and he was very honest with Mommy. He said he might help my "muscle-tone" with a powder taken from "the pituitary gland of a young calf." (Those doctors use such *big* words!) I was to take one capsule a day, plus a tonic of "B-12," to increase my appetite. He said that that would help.

But my heart, he was sure, couldn't be helped. He said he believed that when I was born, a few of the heart cells didn't close properly, and left a hole. Three or four months of the pituitary gland extract might help me to get up on my feet and walk, but my heart—no.

Mommy took me out in the city square to see the pigeons. Ah, that was good! I loved to see them leap up into the air so fast, and spread their wings, and glide all around, so high up, wild and free and beautiful, against the deep blue of the sky and the big white fleecy clouds. I reached out my hands to touch them up there, and I thought, "How wonderful it will be when I get my wings back . . ."

Sorry, Father. I guess I was getting a little impatient.

AFTER we got home, Mommy decided it was time for Cau-Cau to take a little vacation; she needed it, for she'd been with me since I was four months old. Mommy had three week's rest now, from her television work, so she could take care of me, all by herself. She figured she and I would have a wonderful time together, in those three weeks . . . and we did!

It was hard for her, because my brothers and sisters needed her, too, but she made out all right. She sang to me a lot, during those three weeks, and she told me often that I belonged to You. And she prayed. I'd never heard her pray like that, before. One day she said to You:

"God, is it Your purpose to heal my baby? If it is, I'll use that healing to Your glory, and all the rest of my life I'll tell people about it, everywhere I go.

"But if that isn't Your will, and what You want, then give me strength to meet it, Lord. Strength to face the future and to finish what Robin has started in all our hearts in this house, strength to get her Message across to the world. Just strength, Lord, for whatever You have decided."

Sometimes, she would beg You please to let her stay on earth until You had called me Home, so she could watch over me. That thought seemed to haunt her; it was in her heart, like a sharp knife. The idea of my being alone, without her, made her almost terrified.

Many times, Mommy was asked to write articles for the "magazines," on her faith in You, regarding me. She always said, "I will when the time comes." Unconsciously, she was waiting for Your will to be done. She was waiting to see whether I'd be healed Down There or Up Here—whether I was to find my joy on earth or in heaven. It was right that she should wait, for now that I've left earth, she has a great chance to tell a great story about—Us.

Before long, it was Easter. That's a great time, Down There. They "dress up" especially for the Easter service at church, and people go to church then even if they don't go any other time, and I guess that's good, isn't it? They go all week long before Easter Sunday, too, to celebrate the Crucifixion and the Resurrection, and there is something real holy about Holy Week. It seems so sad on Good Friday, and then suddenly it's so bright and glorious on Easter, when Your Son rose from the dead. Some of the people are pretty heedless about it, but the meaning of eternal life gets hold of them, and they're quieter, and better. I think that idea—that I'd go on living in a better condition than I was in then, and that everything would work out all right—I think that idea was strong in Mommy and Daddy and in the whole family, that last Easter I had Down There.

Mommy wheeled me out in my "go-cart," to watch Cheryl and Linda and Dusty hunt for Easter eggs. The "bunny" was supposed to have left them—and Daddy looked at me and said I looked just like the bunny, because my knitted cap was white with big ears on the sides. He got that camera out again . . . !

It was warm now, and Mommy would take me into the shallow part of our swimming pool. That water was wonderful. Mommy would hold my arms around her neck, and I'd kick out, like a little frog, spattering water all over Cau-Cau. She didn't mind. She loved me. I heard her say many times, "God is good to have made her so beautiful."

Beautiful? I guess I was, although when I was born nobody would have thought it, except maybe my parents. Isn't it funny, Father, that the first thing people worried about was my slanted eyes—and by the time I was a year old they were saying, "Hasn't she beautiful eyes?" It's like You say, "All things shall be changed." Even ugly things have a way of changing into beautiful things, under Your hand.

Nurse told us that a friend had said to her, "Never admit that her condition was diagnosed as Mongoloid, because even if she turns out all right, people will never give her a chance." But— I was *changed*, and nobody was thinking of me as "Mongoloid," but just as a beautiful child. They would look at me and say, "She's a doll," or, "She's like a little bird . . . Robin certainly was the name for her."

Mommy named me Elizabeth—after John the Baptist's mother—and Robin, after a pretty little Chinese singer they met once, and when I was born the little Chinese girl was so pleased that she sent me the sweetest little Chinese pajamas and slippers. Too bad we never met.

Speaking of that name, Robin, and birds, . . . whenever I heard bright and sparkling music, like birds singing, I would forget myself and try to fly! I missed my wings so much on earth, and I was so disappointed when I would flap my arms, and get nowhere.

But it was good, even though I had no wings. Some of them didn't know how good it was. Mommy heard once that some doctor had said that babies who came into the world in my condition should be lined up in a row and "machine-gunned," because they were no good to themselves or to anybody else. Father, if that remark was really made, forgive him, for he knows not what he's saying. I wish he could meet You. . . .

BEFORE Cau-Cau came back from her vacation, Mommy, Daddy, and Dusty took me back to see the San Francisco doctor. That trip was a "pistol," as Daddy says. Was there trouble!

They put me in a "lower berth," in my bed-strap, and Dusty was in the berth above me. Mommy slept in the bed right across from me, and Daddy was in the bunk above hers. I was pretty restless during the night, but as soon as I had my breakfast, things quieted down. Dusty and I had fun looking out of the window at northern California; his eyes were as big as saucers.

A minister friend of Daddy's met us at the station, and he took Dusty off for a ride on the "cable cars," and they took me to the hotel. I didn't do so well—I was nervous, and the hotel noises and the taxicab horns kept me from sleeping, and I had another "spell." The night after we saw the doctor, I kept my parents up all night.

They took turns walking me up and down the room. Finally, Daddy lay down on his bed, exhausted; he put me on his chest and patted my back and sang to me and mumbled words, trying to comfort me. Early in the morning my temperature shot up, and they sent for the doctor; he gave me a shot of "penicillin," and something to put me to sleep.

On the train going home, Mommy was up seven times in the night. I was sure glad to get back to my own little bed, in Encino. Mommy and Daddy were there, too; they were so quiet! The doctor told them that my "muscle tone" was better, but my heart was getting worse.

My muscles *were* stronger. I could turn over in my bed, and I could even get on my hands and knees and hold myself in a crawling position. I had eight big teeth and I could chew crackers, which I called "cack-cack." (You see, my tongue was under better control, too.)

I had always had trouble trying to hold up my milk bottle. It was so heavy. Mommy and Ginny got a little perfume bottle, sterilized it and put a nipple on it, and it was so light that I could hold it in my own hands and drain it dry. Of course, my bones were tiny and weak, and there was still that soft spot on my head, which hadn't quite closed. I was tired most of the time, and they had trouble waking me up after my naps in the afternoon. I weighed seventeen pounds, five ounces— not much for a baby nearly two years old!

Cau-Cau took a day a week off now (she needed it!), and on the days when Mommy was working, I was alone with Ginny and Dusty. We had a great time, playing around on the floor of my house. Dusty would hide under my bed, and tease me. He was my favorite; while I couldn't talk to him, we always sort of knew what we were *trying* to say to each other. There was kind of a spark between us, Father, if You know what I mean.

Mommy never forgot what they told her when

I was born—that I couldn't live very long. She was so anxious to be with me during the time I was on earth that she refused to fly in airplanes, on their trips. She was afraid she might "crash," and from the day I was born she had not put her foot in a plane. You put her to quite a test, with that flying business.

There were some big religious meetings being held down in Houston, Texas, and Mommy and Daddy were asked to come and speak. Daddy went, but Mommy was afraid—afraid to *fly*, and she had to fly to get there on time. She let Daddy go, and she tossed all night in her bed, and in her sleep she heard You asking her, "Which comes first—Robin or Me?" It was a hard decision to make.

In the morning, she leaped out of bed and called the airport and made a reservation, and went off to Houston. I think that was the greatest victory of all, on my whole mission—helping Mommy conquer *fear*. She was never afraid to go where You sent her, after that. She knew it was more important to tell the world about what You were doing for her and for me, than to stay in my room night and day.

She flew down to Texas again, shortly after this, to see my grandfather, who was sick. While she was there, You did it again: You led her out to a babies' home called Hope Cottage, in Dallas, where You had little Mary waiting to take my place. Mommy saw Mary while she was walking around the cottage—a little black-eyed baby, with blacker hair, who raised herself up on her elbows and watched Mommy walk around the room. She never took her eyes off Mommy; it was as though she were saying to herself, "Well! At last, you've come!" Mommy couldn't take her eyes off Mary, either. Mommy found out that Mary was part Choctaw Indian, and that struck a spark. Daddy was part Choctaw Indian, too!

Mommy came back and told Daddy she sure hoped that little baby would find a good home, with somebody, and I almost laughed out loud. I knew all about the home she was going to find: it was part of the Plan.

Mary's with them now, Father. I wish I could go Down There again, and visit them. I'd like to see Mommy happy again, like she was the day I got my first tooth. I think I'll send word down to them to change Mary's name to "Doe"; there's something Choctaw about "Doe."

Daddy said he knew Dusty would like having Mary—or Doe—around, because Dusty was getting tired of being the youngest in the family—of being "low man on the totem pole" in our family. It will be good for Dusty, all right. He is "all boy and full of vinegar," but he was kind and tender with Your Littlest Angel—meaning me. It was something, just to watch him go out of his way, more and more, to help me.

I saw that thoughtfulness developing in all the children in "the house of Rogers." On my birthday, Dusty took one of his best toys and wrapped it up in nice tissue paper, and gave it to me. Linda prayed for me. She said the grace at meals, and the grace always included something about me. The night I left to come back Up Here, Linda went to Mommy and said, "I prayed for Robin in Church this morning," and that gave Mommy a great lift. And she was always praying for Nancy, too.

Take good care of Linda, won't you, Father? She's so unselfish; she wants to be a nurse when she grows up, so she can help people—people like me. Cheryl is sweet, too; she wants to be an actress, but Mommy wants her to be a good Christian first, and Mommy knows that being an actress is a dangerous business. There are so many pitfalls. But I think Cheryl will make it, all right. She's got what it takes—You.

I was sorry to leave them, as I watched them becoming more and more unselfish, and doing more and more for people who were weaker than they were. We did quite a job on those children, Father; they learned a great lesson, and they'll never forget it.

WELL, we're getting near the end of my story.

Things began to happen fast Mommy and Daddy had to go to New York, to appear in a rodeo, and they dreaded that, because it meant leaving me, and I was getting no better. Mommy was in such a troubled state of mind that she couldn't settle down to getting her songs ready for the show, and she kept worrying about me and about Cau-Cau, who was tired out. What should she do? Go to New York? Let Cau-Cau go, and stay with me night and day herself? Or what?

Everybody was uneasy, and restless. Cau-Cau worried over my failure to walk. She worked so hard with me, exercising my legs, and when the "orthopedic" man told her it would be at least six months more before I could walk, she almost cried. Mommy decided Cau-Cau had had enough, and that she should leave me, for her own sake.

They both cried when Cau-Cau went away. Poor Cau-Cau kept rubbing my legs until the very day she left us. I wanted so to tell her never to mind, that I would soon be using wings instead of my poor feet, but I couldn't. It was awful, Father, seeing her turn away from me for the last time, but I'm glad now that she went. That last night would have been just too hard for her.

The other children, all of a sudden, got the mumps—and so did I! One side of my face swelled up and then went down, and then the other side swelled up, much worse, and before anybody could do anything, the fever hit my brain.

Two doctors came and worked hard over me; they did their best, but of course it wasn't any good. Late Saturday afternoon they took my temperature; it was 106.

Mommy called in one of the doctors who had been in the hospital the day I was born, and he gave me medicine to kill the pain, and he told Mommy that I cried so because I had a terrific headache.

Mommy and Daddy walked up and down, up and down, outside my little house. Daddy said, "God will call her, when He's ready. We've just *got* to trust Him." The doctor came out and told them that I might go in a matter of seconds now. My kind of heart gave no warning, and they must be ready. . . .

He told Mommy that she and Daddy had done the right thing in keeping me at home, loving me like they had. His own wife was going to have a little baby soon, he said, and if it were a baby like me, he would do the same thing.

Babies like me must have left their mark on him, for he said something You must love, Father, he said that he was going to theological school to equip himself, spiritually, so that he could be of more help to the parents of other problem babies like me. We really helped him, didn't We? Being with me will make him a better doctor with every patient he has from now on! It's good *he* didn't want to "machine-gun" me, like that other doctor!

Late Sunday afternoon, my fever was 108; the doctor told Mommy that I had "mumps encephalitis," and that it was a bad development. Only one child out of nine developed encephalitis, and it was very, very dangerous. He didn't give them much hope that I'd recover from it.

Part of the time when I was conscious, I could see them dimly, all around me. Most of the time I was reaching up for Your arms, Father, for I knew You were very near now. I knew You were coming.

Mommy came in and kissed my hand, and she noticed the funny, rattling way I was breathing; she looked grief-stricken, but there was a sort of peace on her face when she turned and went out on the porch.

My special pal, the dog, Lana, was out there. She kept walking up and down, up and down, restlessly, and then she began to bark, loud and insistently. Lana knew! Mommy patted her while she prayed a prayer of thanksgiving to You for letting me stay two years. Just as Daddy met her on the porch and she went crying into his arms, You came, and I felt myself being lifted up.

What a moment that was! Everything was bright with light, and there was a sound like the rustling of a million angel's wings, and there was singing everywhere. My old clay shell just fell off, and my heart began beating strong and steady, and my head didn't hurt any more.

Well, that's it, Father. That's what happened Down There. That's how I delivered Your message, and I'm sure they got it. They learned, for one thing, that there are many mansions, or "rooms," in Your earthly house—that there's a room for the strong and a room for the sick, a room for the healthy and a room for the weak, a room for those born with ten talents, and a room for those with only one, a room for the rich and a room for the poor. A room for *everyone*, and something for them to do in that room for You. In Your house Down There are many rooms, where we study and teach and get ready to move into Your big light room Up Here.

We did pretty well in that room in my little house, Father. We taught them to see purpose in pain, and messages on the crosses they have to carry around. You know, when Daddy sings now in his big rodeo show, he has a lot of big spotlights making a cross in the centre of the arena. It's sort of a symbol of what's happened to him and to Mommy: the cross has become the great big thing in the middle of their lives. Everything else in their lives now sort of moves around it, like a wheel around a hub.

They're a lot stronger, since they got Our message. There's a new glory inside them and on everything all around them, and they've made up their minds to give it to everybody they meet. The sun's a lot brighter in Encino, since we stopped off there for a while.

And now, Father, please . . . could I just go out and try my wings?